# SPEECH IN THE
PULPIT

# SPEECH IN THE PULPIT

BY

## P. E. SANGSTER

M.A. (Cantab.), L.R.A.M. (Speech and Drama)
Gold Medallist (L.A.M.D.A.)

PHILOSOPHICAL LIBRARY
NEW YORK

PUBLISHED, 1958, BY
PHILOSOPHICAL LIBRARY, INC.
15 EAST 40TH STREET, NEW YORK 16, N.Y.

PRINTED IN GREAT BRITAIN FOR PHILOSOPHICAL LIBRARY
BY ROBERT MACLEHOSE AND CO. LTD
THE UNIVERSITY PRESS, GLASGOW

For
Margaret, my Mother
and
Mary, my Wife

# *Preface*

IT would be ungrateful to omit mention of the debt I owe to a number of kind friends.

Miss Eleanor Pearson-Littlewood, LRAM, was kind enough to read the manuscript and make a number of helpful suggestions. Dr C. W. Towlson, MA, BD, also examined the work critically, made several valuable points which I gladly incorporated, and gave his seal of approval to the work, a seal I treasure.

Miss Margaret Gregory, of her kindness, spent many hours of her leisure typing the manuscript, and Keith Roome helped prepare it.

My father, the Rev. Dr W. E. Sangster, MA, has been, in this as in all else, the greatest help of all.

ASHVILLE COLLEGE        P.E.S.
HARROGATE

# *Contents*

# Foreword

I AM glad Mr Sangster has written this book. I wish I could have studied it—for reading it through is not enough —forty-five years ago, when I was a student at Richmond Theological College. Recently a listener to me on a wireless programme wrote to say, 'With a voice like that you should not be allowed to broadcast.' I remembered and quoted in my reply a famous answer of one to whom I owe so much, the late Rev. Dr Russell Maltby, to whom an objector wrote in similar strain. Characteristically Dr Maltby replied: 'Be thankful you can switch off. I have to live with that voice always.'

Pleasantry aside, much pulpit work is lessened in value by those errors in voice-production, enunciation, those distracting mannerisms and other deviations which are dealt with in this ably written book.

Mr Sangster contents himself with a brief paragraph on the prayers from the pulpit. He says modestly that they are so individual and personal that 'it borders on effrontery to mention them at all'. Yet I wish he had done so, for the prayers, badly expressed and badly spoken, can be the most boring part of a service. The tradition in most of the Free Churches calls for extempore prayer. Yet who has not been bored by a verbal tour of the world? Who has not heard God being grossly misinformed about the current political and social situation? Who has not noted the unexpectancy of prayers like, 'Bless all who are sick and make them well,' realizing, as surely the thoughtful worshipper must, that if one ward full of patients, in one hospital in one town, were thus made well, by dinner-time it would be incredible headline news for days in all the newspapers of the world. I can never understand why it is considered so praiseworthy to prepare carefully what we speak to men on behalf of God, and to trust to the inspiration of the moment to speak to God on behalf of men. And when the 'extempore prayer' is moaned in a flat, dull voice, it is a grey monotony which is only followed by the preacher. Everyone else is secretly thinking of something more interesting, and it is a relief to sit up and hunt for the collection sixpence. I should have thought it reasonable to argue that speaking to God was a far greater responsibility than speaking to men, especially speaking to God on behalf of other people. There is a strong case, in my view, for the careful preparation of a number of brief prayers, or the use of classic forms, such as some of the Collects of the Prayer Book offer. But, of course, all public praying can be ruined by the faults Mr Sangster is trying to correct.

A fresh, well-produced, *interesting* voice which yet does not draw attention to itself is an enormous asset to a preacher. To help him possess this asset Mr Sangster has written this book and I commend it and wish it every success. If it succeeds, thousands of listeners will benefit.

LESLIE D. WEATHERHEAD

THE CITY TEMPLE

LONDON

# CHAPTER I

# By Way of Introduction

IF you believed the old fallacy that a voice is a gift of God and that there is little or nothing we can do about it, then you would not be reading this book. So you begin well. You admit that a voice can be trained.

It is a great pity that speech training has been the Cinderella of the curriculum both in schools and colleges. It is assumed—dangerous assumption!—that though we study theology hard, and work for hours preparing our sermons, the delivery of the sermon will look after itself.

We have all suffered from listening to a poor voice. The message may be a fine one, the illustrations apposite, the speaker brimming with enthusiasm, but if we cannot hear him, or can only hear him with difficulty, or are constantly jarred by bad tone or an irritating vocal habit which could be cured by only a little knowledge and patience, then what is the good of it all? How often have we felt, though forborne, to say: 'What a waste! If only he had a better voice!'

Voices with serious impediments are happily rare, and Churches do not accept preachers with such defects. So every preacher in this country *could* have, if not a great voice, at least one which people can hear and understand. Since 'it pleased God by the foolishness of preaching to save them that believe', then surely it is our duty to prepare ourselves to that end. Our preparation lacks much that is important if it does not include the very means by which the message is to be made known.

I have heard the story—though I cannot vouch for its truth—that some two generations ago a visitor went to a

theological college and asked the Principal, in the course
of conversation, what the men were doing. 'They are
preparing their sermons', was the answer. 'Most of them
are writing, but Mr —— is no doubt practising the word
"ra-a-a-diancy" in front of a mirror.' The Principal
really said it in amusement, but that student became one
of the most distinguished preachers of the century. I have
read some of this distinguished man's published works
and they border on the banal: it was his magnificent voice
which made his reputation. If the mere effect of the voice
has so great a power to command the faith, how blame-
worthy we are if we do not make full use of it.

I think it would be difficult to exaggerate the importance
of speech-training for preachers. 'Why is it', asked an
ecclesiastic of David Garrick, 'that I, who speak great
truths, can only fill my church once a week, while you,
who speak merely fiction, can fill a theatre every night?'
'Because', replied the actor, 'you speak truth as if it were
fiction, while I speak fiction as if it were truth.' We are
to learn to speak truth as if it *is* truth—and, in the end,
the only truth that really matters. It is but little trouble to
take, when we consider the greatness of our cause.

How shall we begin? First, by finding out what our
voice sounds like. One obvious way is to hear it on a tape-
recorder. This may result in a shock, but it is a shock we
expect our congregations to endure! The better way,
however, since our concern is with what our congregations
think, is to ask somebody. A wife or husband is hardly
suitable. Domestic peace might be shattered for years
by the comment: 'Ghastly!' Alternatively, connubial devotion may be blind; the reply 'Wonderful!' might be true
for the speaker but false for anybody else. Ask a close
friend of the same sex, preferably another preacher.

'What do I sound like?' Here, as a suggestion, is a list of questions which may help in this inquiry.

> Am I audible? Too soft? Too loud?
>
> Is my voice clear? Muffled?
>
> Is my tone good? Firm? Wobbly? Full? Thin? Free? Hard?
>
> Is my voice nasal? Is it hoarse?
>
> Do I enunciate clearly?
>
> Is there sufficient variety in my pitch? Is it monotonously on one note?
>
> Do I vary the pace? Do I pause sufficiently? Do I gabble? Am I ponderously slow?
>
> Do I vary the volume?
>
> Do I appear to patronize the congregation?
>
> Am I immobile? Can I move with effect?
>
> Do I carry conviction? Do I sound as if I mean what I say?
>
> Do I look convincing? Apologetic?

It is my hope to find the cause and cure for each defect suggested in the table. It will be necessary first to consider the technicalities of speech-training, but only in outline. Before that, however, let us consider the all-important question of the mental approach.

# CHAPTER II

# The Approach

MOST of us have bad attacks of 'nerves' before we go into the pulpit. Up to a point, this can be a help. The feeling of nervousness pitches us to a high performance, tenses us to speak well. Beyond that point, however, the 'nerves' are a serious handicap; they are better called fright. There is a difference. Nervousness keys us up; fright paralyses: nervousness ensures our best; fright ensures our worst: nervousness comes of a realization that God has given us a great task; fright comes of a suspicion that we are not equal to it.

When we are very nervous, the muscles of the body instinctively tauten, and the whole frame becomes rigid. The chest is held tightly, and the throat is stiff. The effect on our speech is disastrous. It is from the chest that we breathe, and any rigidity there inevitably spoils the voice. If we are cramped in our breathing, we are cramped in our speech; breath is liable to come in choked gasps and the tone will probably be thin, shrill and quavering. Stiffness in the throat is worse, for any loss of resilience in the larynx will lead to harsh or hoarse tone. The reaction of the congregation is automatic. We feel ill at ease and look it; we sound it. 'Poor fellow! Better not invite him again!'

How can we attain the ease of mind that makes for easy delivery? By prayer, especially that kind of prayer in which we recall the fact that God called us to be preachers and is with us all the time. This will give us confidence. God would not have called us to be preachers, to proclaim His Word, if we had not been, at least potentially, worthy of the calling. Since He has done so, we must have confidence both in God and in the message He gives.

With the ease of mind which these thoughts can give us, we should be able to have ease of body also. How? The answer is *relaxation*. Let anybody try to give of his best with his body held rigid. He cannot. Yet we often attempt to do so in the pulpit.

The correct position for speaking is this: heels two or three inches apart, the whole body resting evenly on the legs. Above the hips, the body should be as relaxed as possible. Stomach and seat should be tucked in, the chest well forward, and the head resting lightly and held high. Arms should be at the sides, completely relaxed; shoulders should be back and the whole body erect. This, then, is the basic position for preaching. It suggests confidence; it rests all weight easily and evenly on both legs, so allowing the rest of the body to relax.

Here are exercises for relaxation:
(1) Lie on your back on the floor or a couch and form a mental picture of floating on water or lying on a cloud. Begin to drift off to sleep and feel all your muscles relax.
(2) Take up the same position and ask a friend to test you. If he pulls your big toe hard and your head doesn't shake, you are not relaxed!
(3) Walk in a good upright position easily about the room, stopping in the correct position every few paces. Make a good speaking position a habit.

Here is an exercise for taking up the correct speaking position: Place your feet as I have suggested, raise the arms high above the head, stretch up and then fall forward limply; slowly uncurl into the correct position.

If you imagine that these exercises are too elementary for you and of minor importance, then consider this—

B

that *relaxation* is the first essential of good speech, and that actors in training spend a very considerable time doing just this, learning to relax.

If the body is relaxed, harsh tone can become round and pleasing, a thin voice can become a full one, delivery that was an effort can become a pleasure, and what was hard, easy.

The mental approach, therefore, leads us from the spiritual ease of mind to the severely practical ease of body. The first comes by prayer, the second by practice.

We must now briefly consider the technicalities of voice production.

# CHAPTER III

# *Breathing*

CORRECT breathing is fundamental to good speech, and a study of it logically follows the achievement of relaxation.

We use three types of breathing for different purposes.

In repose—during sleep and in normal conversation.

In action—notably, for us, in public speaking.

In great effort—such as an athlete must employ during a hard run.

Two areas of our bodies are involved in breathing.

The Chest. Our lungs, the power behind speech, are surrounded by the chest-bone and ribs at the front and sides, and by the spine at the back.

The Diaphragm, a saucer-shaped sheet of muscle which separates the chest-area from the abdomen.

In the first kind of breathing, the area used is the diaphragm, with only a little help from the chest. This type of breathing is really reflexive. We enlarge the area of the lungs vertically by the contraction (flattening) of the diaphragm and so inhale. As we exhale, the diaphragm moves upwards and so diminishes the area of the lungs.

In the third type of breathing, the top of the chest is employed in addition to the central chest and diaphragm.

It is with the second type of breathing, however, that we are concerned. To breathe correctly, we must train ourselves to control absolutely breathing in the centre of the chest. Maximum lung expansion is permitted by the raising of the lower ribs; as we breathe in, the ribs move forward and upward. We must encourage the forward movement but resist the upward one. Breathing from the top of the chest is wasteful of energy and ugly to watch; breathing from the abdomen alone is also wasteful and ugly (the diaphragm will look after itself; exercises which could lead to a bulging abdomen are not to be encouraged); correct breathing is *central breathing*.

Here is the basic exercise for all breathing:

(1) Relax.
(2) Take up a good position.
(3) Place the backs of the finger-tips against the lower ribs.
(4) Open the mouth loosely and expand the chest. (I deliberately avoid saying 'breathe in'; we should take the breath in unconsciously.)
(5) Feel the expansion.
(6) Exhale slowly.

*Do not*

(a) Raise the shoulders.
(b) Strain in any way: the exercise should be almost effortless.

*Do*

(a) Forget about breathing in; just expand the ribs.
(b) Breathe in through the mouth and nose, out through the mouth.
(c) Make sure that the sides and back of the chest are also expanding.

There is an infinite number of variations on this exercise. Our aim is, since this is important in preaching, to inhale very quickly and silently and exhale as slowly as possible. Any variation which assists this is a good one, but we must remember never to strain.

The practised speaker, holding, as he must, his chest well forward, is able to speak quite a long sentence on the outgoing breath, before a full stop, or some other pause allows him to collapse his lungs and refill them quickly.

If we have learnt to relax and breathe correctly, we are prepared to do real justice to our next consideration—Tone.

# CHAPTER IV

## *Tone*

THE note is made in the vocal cords in the larynx. Provided these are not misused, they will look after themselves,

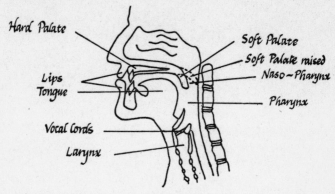

and we need not study them. The commonest misuse, however, is to try to force power from the larynx. We cannot do this, and the result is bad tone. The way to avoid it is never to speak from the throat. Good full tone comes with ease; with effort comes thin tone.

The note, on its passage from the larynx, then acquires tone from the resonators. These, working upwards, are:

The pharynx.
The mouth.
The nose and naso-pharynx.
Various cells and sinuses higher up.

The mouth, being the largest and most mobile, is by far the most important of these. Our voices differ, basically, because we differ both in the structure of this all-important resonator, and in our use of it. In a later chapter, we shall consider briefly the shape of our mouth while we are making different sounds, so that we can confirm this. Meanwhile, we must consider what we require of tone.

First, it should be *full*. Full tone has roundness and body. It is neither restrainedly thin nor harsh through forcing power.

Second, it should be both *firm* and *free*. These, obviously, are contradictory, but it is the balance between firmness and freedom that we desire. Too firm a voice is hard; too free a voice is woolly. Our tone must be firm, but not granite; free, but not hysterical.

Third, it should be *forward*. We have already noted that speaking from the throat is harmful to the vocal cords. The voice should consciously be from the front of the mouth, from the lips and teeth and tongue. Here we should make a conscious effort, which will then become habit, of speaking from the front. Harsh tone is the inevitable result of speaking from the throat.

If we find difficulty in making tone forward by a conscious effort, we can force ourselves to produce it by using a syllable which begins on the lips and contains a forward vowel, e.g. 'mee' or 'moo'. Vowel sounds can be ruined by a lack of forward tone, e.g. $\bar{a}$, a beautiful sound, becomes constricted and nasal if not kept forward, *au* becomes nasal and, in the North, flattened to an ugly $\bar{a}$.

Fourth, it should be *fluid*. All public speaking should be, not in staccato bursts, but in a stream. It should not be sing-song. It should have an underlying music that does not predominate, but accompanies the sense, phrase by phrase, and sentence by sentence.

Fifth, it should be *flexible*. It should be possible for the practised preacher to vary the pitch, pace and volume of his voice without losing tone. The man who, at the dramatic moment of his illustration, drops his voice to a whisper which comes across to the congregation as a harsh croak, is not in full control of his tone.

If you feel that your voice lacks any of these essentials of good tone, here is your way to cure it.

(1) If you feel your voice lacks *fullness*
    (*a*) Make sure you are breathing correctly.
    (*b*) Practise all the vowel sounds, especially the long $\bar{o}$ and $\bar{a}$.

(2) If you lack *firmness*
    (*a*) Make sure you have the confidence you need.
    (*b*) Practise the explosive consonants.
    (*c*) Exaggerate your articulation.
    (*d*) Bite on the words at the front of your mouth.

(3) If you lack *freedom*
    (*a*) Relax.
    (*b*) Read passages to yourself that require very sensitive reading, such as the story of Ruth and Naomi; and then read them aloud gently.

(4) If you lack the ability to speak *forward*, the only cure is to think yourself consciously into doing it. This can come with practice.

(5) If you lack *fluidity*
    (*a*) Practise reciting poetry with a jog-trot metre that *forces* you to make the words flow.
    (*b*) Practise reading in short phrases, feeling the flow of the words.

(6) If you lack *flexibility*, be comforted. So do most people! This only comes with long practice and observance of the other rules of speech-training.

Now on to the speech-sounds themselves.

# CHAPTER V

## Speech Sounds

### VOWELS

A VOWEL is a speech-sound made by the free, unobstructed passage of air.

Generally speaking, it is in vowel sounds that local dialects are heard, and this makes a problem. Do we want to eradicate dialect? Do we want all to conform to the same vowel sounds? Most people would give a categorical 'No' to these questions, but it is not as easy as that. There is, for instance, the problem of intelligibility. Out of his own locality, many a possessor of a broad accent simply would not be understood. Further, even when voices are understood, incorrect vowel sounds can make congregations writhe. For instance, to a Yorkshireman, the Cockney 'līdee' for 'lady' would probably be as annoying as his own 'lairdi' would be to the Londoner. Finally, there is often something comic in a particular dialect to people who do not use it. The genius of a succession of Lancashire comedians, for instance, has made the very hint of the accent a signal for laughter. No preacher can afford to be unintelligible, or irritating, or comic. On these grounds I do not think we can afford to use broad dialects in the pulpit, unless we are content never to leave our own locality, where none of these objections could apply. If we are likely to travel about, then we should be wise to eradicate all trace of dialect from our vowels. What is left of it after the vowels are corrected will be found neither unintelligible, nor irritating, nor comic, and may well, on the contrary, lend a certain 'character' and piquancy to a voice.

There is, however, a further problem. It is rare for a man who constantly mispronounces a vowel to be aware of it. Even when it is pointed out, custom has made him incapable of hearing it. What hope, then, has he of curing a vowel fault from a table of vowel sounds? Frankly, very little. If you have, or suspect you have, a vowel fault, you need to hear it correctly, together with the incorrect sound you have been making. Then you will be in a position to correct it for yourself by practice.

Here is the way to go about it:

(1) Ask anybody who may reasonably be expected to know (beautifully vague, I know) if you have an incorrect vowel sound.

(2) Get him to give you the correct sound and your own incorrect sound until you can hear the difference.

(3) Check the vowel sound in the table below and make sure you are pronouncing it as the fifth column suggests. Since you *are* pronouncing it wrongly, then you are clearly not doing this.

(4) Practise using the newly learnt vowel-sound in other words until it becomes habit.

If you find that all your vowel-sounds are pure—fortunate person!—you can happily ignore the whole section except for the general exercises.

Before we come to the table of vowels, here are some exercises for use in all speech work. They use the basic organs—the jaw, the lips, the teeth, the tongue and the roof of the mouth (at the front, the hard palate; at the back, the soft palate).

(1) Relaxing the jaw. Let the jaw drop repeatedly, feeling the difference between a tense and relaxed jaw.

(2) Lips

    (i) use the lips in forward positions and loosen them.

    (ii) practise fast nonsense phrases, especially those containing sounds formed on the lips, e.g.:

        (*a*) Peter Piper picked a peck of pickled peppercorn.

        (*b*) Five feverish finches fought fiendishly for fifteen Fridays.

        (*c*) By a babbling brook burbled a bevy of bibulous baboons.

        (*d*) We wore worn-out tweeds, which were worse than widow's weeds.

        (*e*) Many marmosets murmured amusingly of their matrimonial memories.

(3) Tongue-tip and roof of mouth. Flick the tongue in and out, pointing it, and then flick it alternately behind the upper and lower teeth.

(4) Back of tongue and roof of mouth. Arch the spade of the tongue high against the soft palate. Alternately arch and flatten.

Now for the chart of vowel-sounds. This may require just a little explanation. Vowel sounds are not, unfortunately, merely the written A, E, I, O and U. They are here divided into monophthongs, in which a single sound is made and diphthongs, in which two sounds are made. Monophthongs are further divided into open (or long) and shut (or short) vowels.

The position for all vowel sounds is as follows:

    (*a*) Front teeth about 1″ apart.

    (*b*) Tongue tip against the base of the lower teeth.

    (*c*) The soft palate raised.

It is in the shape of the lips and the position of the tongue that the vowel-sounds differ.

| Sound | Word as Example | Open/Shut | Type | Position | Comment |
|---|---|---|---|---|---|
| ā | hard | Open | Monophthong | Lips relaxed and well open. | — |
| ōō | pool | ,, | ,, | Lips pouted, well forward. Very small round opening. | Mispronounced when the tongue is too high. |
| ēē | seal | ,, | ,, | Tongue arches at back. Lips relaxed. Wide narrow opening. | Often wrongly made a diphthong, as ī+ēē in Cockney. |
| au | taught | ,, | ,, | Lips pouted forward and in △ shape. Well open. | Often mispronounced when ending in 'r' e.g. 'sower' for 'saw'. |
| er | fern | ,, | ,, | Lips relaxed. Moderately open. | — |
| ă | fat | Shut | ,, | Blade of tongue raised slightly. | Affected speech tends to make the sound ĕ. Northern version very clipped. |
| ŏŏ | pull | ,, | ,, | Lips same shape as ōō but not so pouted and a little wider. | |
| ĭ | ship | ,, | ,, | As ēē, but opening less wide. | Final 'y' as in pity often made long incorrectly, as 'pitēē' for 'pitĭ'. |
| ŏ | hot | ,, | ,, | Lips in △ shape. Moderately open. | Affected speech makes this au, as in 'awf' for 'off'. This is accepted by dictionaries but not by congregations. |
| ŭ | bun | ,, | ,, | Blade of tongue raised slightly. | Not used in broad Northern speech, where ōō is substituted. Southern speech makes this 'băn'. |
| ĕ | met | ,, | ,, | Blade raised a little higher. | — |

| | | | | |
|---|---|---|---|---|
| ĕ+ĭ | male | Diphthong | — | Frequently mispronounced Monophthong in Scotland. Both sounds dragged in North. In Cockney is ā+ĭ. |
| ŏ+ŏŏ | rope | ,, | — | ŏ is midway between au and ŏ. North pronounces au+ŏŏ. Cockney is ä+ŏŏ. |
| ä+ĭ | file | ,, | — | 'Refained' speech makes this ä+ĭ. Cockney very broad ä. ä should be midway between ä and ä. |
| ā+ŏŏ | loud | ,, | — | Many variations. Cockney leaves out the second half of the diphthong. Birmingham uses nasal ĕ+ŏŏ. |
| au+ĭ | boil | ,, | — | The first sound is light. It is between au and ŏ, but nearer au. |
| ĭ+ŏŏ | mute | ,, | — | Regarded by some as not a diphthong, but the intrusion of the consonant 'y'. Be careful not to make first sound 'ēē'. |

Many authorities complicate vowel-tables by classifying sounds ending in 'r'. In fact, at the end of a word, 'r' often has a dual purpose. In addition to its obvious consonantal value, it throws back before it a hint of a vowel sound, which cannot be shown as any of the vowels so far demonstrated.

In addition to all the vowel sounds shown, there exists in English the 'neutral' vowel, a sound with no strict definition, which is used where the merest approximation to a vowel sound is needed. It is represented by the symbol ə. I have underlined several in the following sentence.

'He oft<u>e</u>n said th<u>a</u>t he preferred to live near <u>a</u> city like London.'

It would sound ridiculous to pronounce these sounds any other way, e.g. 'He of-t<u>e</u>n said that. . . .'

The neutral vowel also occurs in words ending with the letter 'r', such as 'pair', which becomes the diphthong ĕ + ə, and 'pure', which becomes the triphthong ĭ + o͞o + ə.

## CONSONANTS

A consonant is a speech sound which is interrupted by one or more of the articulative organs. The tables, remember, are for reference and guidance, *not* for absorption by those who do not need their help.

Consonants can be classified in many ways, but for our purpose three are sufficient.

First, there is the division into vocal and aspirate sounds. Make an 's' sound. It is a mere hissing sound, without the voice being used. Now, without moving your lips, teeth or tongue, use you voice in making the same sound. It automatically becomes 'z'. 'S', then, is unvoiced, or aspirate; 'Z' is voiced, or vocal.

Second, there is the division into sustained and explosive sounds. Make the 's' sound again and continue making it; you can sustain the sound. Now try to sustain the sound 'p'; you cannot do it. The sound is made by the explosive parting of the lips—'s' is sustained; 'p' is explosive.

| Voiced Example | Unvoiced | Example | Organs of Formation | Sustained or Explosive | Position of Organ | Comments |
|---|---|---|---|---|---|---|
| Z zeal | S | seal | Tip of tongue and upper gums. | Sustained | Tip of tongue close behind, but not touching, upper teeth. | — |
| V vole | F | foal | Lower lip and upper teeth. | ,, | Tip of tongue behind lower teeth, upper teeth touching lower lip. | — |
| ZH azure | SH | should | Blade of tongue and hard palate. | ,, | As 'z' and 's', but tongue more arched. | — |
| TH then | th | thing | Tip of tongue and teeth. | ,, | Tip of tongue over and touching lower teeth. | — |
| W win | WH | when | Lips. | ,, | Approximation of lips. | — |
| L lake | — | — | Tip of tongue and upper gums. | ,, | Two distinct sounds: see below. | — |
| M more | — | — | Lips. | ,, | Soft palate lowered. Tongue relaxed. | Nasal. |
| N nor | — | — | Tip of tongue and upper gums. | ,, | Soft palate lowered. Tip of tongue touching upper gums. | Nasal. |
| R roar | — | — | ,, | ,, | Three distinct sounds: see below. | — |

| | | | | | | | |
|---|---|---|---|---|---|---|---|
| Y | your | — | — | Front of tongue and hard palate. | Sustained | Sides of tongue blade approach hard palate: tongue grooved. | — |
| NG | hang | — | — | Back of tongue and soft palate. | „ | Soft palate lowered. Back of tongue arched up to meet soft palate. | Nasal |
| | — | H | hot | Open mouth. | „ | — | Not strictly a consonant. |
| B | boy | P | pay | Lips. | Explosive | Tongue relaxed: explosion by lips. | ‖ |
| D | do | T | too | Tip of tongue and upper gums. | „ | Tip of tongue touching upper gums. | |
| G | gale | K | kale | Back of tongue and soft palate. | „ | Back of tongue arched up to meet soft palate. | — |

*COMPOUNDS*
J = D + ZH (jam)
CH = T + SH (church)
X = K + S (expense)
or G + S (exult)
Q = K + W (queer)

Third, consonants can be classified by the way they are formed, by various combinations of the articulative organs, such as tip of tongue and upper gums.

*L Sounds*

There are two in English, clear L and dark L.

Clear L is used before vowels, e.g. 'lake'. Position: tongue arched. Tip of tongue makes quick but definite contact with hard palate.

Dark L is used before consonants and finally, e.g. 'belt', 'roll'. Position: top of tongue hollow and back raised to soft palate. Tip of tongue makes contact with hard palate. Dark L is often incorrectly used for Clear L, especially in London. Worse, Dark L sometimes becomes so 'dark' that it is invisible! In some parts of the country it is omitted.

*R Sounds*

There are three—unrolled R, rolled R, and tapped R.

Unrolled R is used in initial positions e.g. 'rage', 'unreal'. Position: tip of tongue curled up in proximity of the upper gums.

Rolled R is used by Scottish speakers. It is a series of taps by the tongue against the upper gums.

Tapped R is used between vowels and in final position before a following consonant, e.g. 'arrow', 'for always'. Position: the tongue arches and one tap is made by the tongue tip against the upper gums.

*Common defects in Consonants*

*S Sounds*

Lisping. Sometimes 'th' is used for S. In this case the tip of the tongue has protruded too far and time must be spent pushing it back. A pencil can be used for this.

c

A consultation with a dentist might also help, because lisping is often caused by faulty teeth.

## R Sounds

Frequently this sound is not vigorous enough. For 'very' one commonly hears both 've-y' and 'vewy'. The back of the tongue must be lowered and the front raised.

## L Sounds

Especially in the South, a dark L is the only one employed. As the Clear L is one of the most beautiful sounds we use, this is a pity. More vigorous use of the tongue is the cure.

## The Glottal Stop

This is the omission of consonant sounds, e.g. 'I- be-er go and ta- a loo-' for 'I'd better go and take a look'. The cure is to break up the words into syllables. This defect is found all over the country. It may be due to laziness, but since it is often easier to leave the missing sound in, and since it is common both in areas formerly occupied by the Danes and in Denmark today, it may be a linguistic relic. Almost as offensive is:

## Harsh Attack on Initial Vowels

This is a far too vigorous enunciation of sounds such as 'The eyes of the blind shall be opened.' It is done, no doubt, to aid clarity, but it is ugly to hear.

### ARTICULATION AND ENUNCIATION

Articulation is the clear and exact delivery of a sound; it refers chiefly to consonants. Enunciation is the clear and exact delivery of the vowel-sounds. These two, therefore, are the aim of every speaker.

We must steer a middle course between the slovenly speech which cannot with any clarity reach the back of our congregation, and the over-precise speech which is exceedingly annoying. If the speaker is saying, 'Many of you are loyal supporters of our great cause, but others...', this may be heard at the back of the church as 'Men-few - loy - sport - vour - gray caw,- bu- tuth...', or 'Men-nee of yew are loy-al sup-port-ers of ow-er great cause, but others...'. Neither is tolerable, but the first is *much more common*, for laziness seems deeper in our nature than over-zealousness.

If our voices are to reach the back, we must obviously articulate and enunciate more clearly than we do in normal conversation. Further, as we naturally drop our voices in volume and pitch at the ends of phrases and sentences, it is precisely in those places that we must be most careful. I will italicize the danger spots in the sentence already quoted: 'Many of you are loyal suppor*ters* of our great *cause*, but others, who have been here only a short *time*, do not even know what we are *doing*.' Standing well, therefore, we should aim our voices straight at the back of the gallery, to ensure that our every word will carry; we should 'focus' our speech.

Good articulation and enunciation obviously depend on the several excellences of our speech sounds. Here are a few exercises for general use:

(1) Read aloud any passage, deliberately over-emphasizing every sound—vowels first, and then consonants. You may find weaknesses for yourself. You will certainly strengthen the articulative organs.

(2) Take each vowel in turn and give it different initial and final consonants.

(3) Practise saying voiced, and the corresponding un-voiced consonants, alternately.

(4) If you have found faulty vowels or consonants in your own voice, practise the correct and incorrect sounds alternately.

As far as intelligibility is concerned, consonants are much more important than vowels. Here are a few exercises for consonants only, particularly useful for those whose speech is indistinct, or whose voice will not carry (see also Chapter 12):

(1) Speak through the closed teeth such sentences as:

> Five thousand thrushes seemed far too few.
> The dentist drilled for days on end.
> Babies blow bubbles beautifully.

The fact that the teeth are closed forces the articulative organs to function more vigorously. It was a similar method (placing pebbles in his mouth and reducing the number one by one) that enabled Demosthenes, the great orator, to overcome his defect of speech.

(2) A great actor once said—'Make your consonants like pistol-shots'. Whisper any passage. Ask a friend if he can hear every consonantal sound you make.

### PRONUNCIATION

There is, I suppose, little harm in pronouncing 'Socrates' 'Soh-crayts', but it does proclaim ignorance, and a preacher cannot afford to be considered a fool. Nor is there any harm in pronouncing 'cinema' 'ky-nee-mar', as a Professor of my acquaintance does, excusing his pronunciation on the grounds of the word's Greek derivation, but a preacher cannot afford to be considered a pedant. There are only two guides to pronunciation, and both are fallible—common sense and the *Oxford English Dictionary*.

A warning. If you didn't happen to study a foreign language at school (and a large number never got the chance) do not attempt to pronounce words from that language in the pulpit. After a recent school service I attended, I was embarrassed by a number of inquiries about the Rev. ——'s French. Boys, I am afraid, often have a snobbish streak in them: the risk wasn't worth it.

# CHAPTER VI

# *Variation*

THERE are three important things to vary in good speech —pitch, pace, and volume. We shall consider them in that order.

## PITCH

Most people prefer to have a deeper-pitched rather than a higher-pitched voice. In men it may be because a deeper voice sounds more masculine; in women there will doubtless be many reasons that no man could follow! Men also seem to prefer a deeper voice in women. Lear said of Cordelia, 'Her voice was ever soft, gentle and low, an excellent thing in woman', and it is also true that most women who have won fame with their speaking voices have had low ones.

Two things, however, are certain. (1) The pitch of the voice does not matter nearly as much as the quality of the tone. (2) We can do nothing whatever about the pitch of our voice; we must just accept it. If we attempt to make the centre of our range higher than it should be, we sound shrill and apologetic. If we attempt to make it lower, then we sound throaty and melancholy. In both cases we ruin the tone.

We ought to know the centre of our range. That and the few notes above and below it are the ones we commonly use. If we start too high we shall let out a strained squawk when we want to go higher for special effects. If we start too low, then again we can only growl incoherently when special low effects are needed, and we are also liable to raise our pitch (since we can go no lower) at the end of a sentence—with ruinous effect.

Here, roughly are the middle notes of the various voices:

Women.  Soprano: the B above the middle C. Mezzo: a third below the Soprano. Contralto: a third below the Mezzo.

Men.     Tenor: the A below middle C. Baritone: a third below the Tenor. Bass: a third below the Baritone.

Find your own middle note by humming M until it feels easy. Hold the note. Speak a short passage on the same note, gradually moving a little above and below the note until you are sure you have found the centre of your own range.

Now you have established your range, it is most important that you vary your pitch within it, or the result will be monotony. At the same time, you must avoid the other extreme of pitch hysteria.

The voice that never varies in pitch is a tedious one; it is also a common one. Used in a sermon, such a voice may well cure insomnia, but it can serve little other purpose. The 'holy drone' is a term applied to this particular defect. Its causes are probably two. One is intoning. This inevitably leads to lack of variety in pitch, unless the man who intones is aware of the danger and takes conscious steps against it. The other is anxiety (very laudable anxiety) that every word shall be heard. Men sometimes think their voices will have greater clarity if they never vary the pitch. Clarity, however, does not come this way.

Pitch hysteria is the over-compensation indulged in by the man who suspects that his voice does not vary sufficiently in pitch. Accordingly, often in violation of the sense of a passage, the voice plunges wildly about, using the extremes of the range often and pointlessly. I remember hearing a London headmaster reading:

```
And                              char
                          and        it
              faith,                  y.
      now abideth          hope
```

The 'hope' was so low that it was only audible as a growl, and the first half of 'charity' was a very high tenor.

How, then, should we vary our pitch? Some experts have made lists of places at which pitch should change. Sound enough in their way, these rules are of little practical value, since a self-conscious observance of such rules would make the changes worthless. It should be sufficient to be aware of the need for variety in pitch, and to practise reading passages with this in mind.

As an example (not to be used for practice) here is a passage from St John's Gospel 20[15-16], showing the necessity of change of pitch.

'Jesus saith unto her, [1][Woman, why weepest thou? Whom seekest thou? [2][She, supposing him to be the gardener, saith unto him, [3][Sir, if thou have borne him hence, tell me where thou hast laid him, and I will take him away.

[4][Jesus saith unto her, [5][Mary. [6][She turned herself, and saith unto him [7][Rabboni; [8][which is to say, Master.'

Reasons for the change of pitch in order.

[1] Change lower. A man's voice.
[2] Change back to middle pitch.
[3] Change higher. A woman's voice is being suggested.

⁴ Change back to middle pitch.
⁵ Change lower. Strong emotion and a man's voice.
⁶ Change higher. Strong excitement.
⁷ Change very high. Extreme emotion.
⁸ Change. Parenthesis.

Here is another example, taken this time from a sermon. The less dramatic nature of the passage makes fewer changes necessary. '

'We hear no more of the young man who sought eternal life and would not give up his wealth. Perhaps, though it is not recorded, he returned to Christ, all his possessions sold. ¹[I like to think so. ²[Perhaps he was one of those who stood at the foot of the cross, and saw how Christ fulfilled the advice he had given. ³[But we shall never know.

⁴['What the story does tell us, however, is that decency is not enough. Though Jesus loved him, the man went away sad, for in spite of his goodness, he would not give up the one thing which separated him from Christ. ⁵[Christ's demand is absolute.'

¹ Change lower. Hint of parenthesis.
² Change back to middle pitch.
³ Change lower. Hint of parenthesis.
⁴ Change back to middle pitch.
⁵ Change higher. Vital point.

*Inflexion*

This is a subsection of pitch. Pitch refers to the rise or fall of the voice in a passage; inflexion is the rise or fall of the voice within single words. An uninflected voice is dull.

A voice that only employs change of pitch may be represented thus.

with variation of Pitch and Inflexion the correct result is this:

Basic inflexions are straight up and down: 'Who?' (ends on higher note); 'Me' (ends on lower note). Compound inflexions show both directions, the final effect of the inflexion being the direction of the final part. If we wish to show scorn in the question and insistence in the answer, the inflexions will be like this: 'Who?' (fall in the middle: final effect a rise); 'Me' (rise in the middle: final effect a fall). There are, of course, infinite variations on this simple theme; consider Lady Bracknell's famous query in *The Importance of Being Earnest:*

'In a handbag?'

It is important for us to be aware of the necessity of inflexion, to remember that an uninflected voice is dull and an overinflected one very irritating, and to practise by reading a short dialogue passage uninflected, overinflected, and with good inflexion.

Let me give three warnings. First, a downward inflexion normally occurs at the end of every phrase and sentence. Make sure the last word is clearly articulated, or the congregation will not hear it. Second, do not use a *sheer* inflexion. This is a common fault. At the end of a sentence, for instance, many speakers drop their voices, not by a fraction but by many notes. The last sound is then only audible as a growl. It is advisable to prepare for a final note by a rising inflexion near the end, so that the

last note is not lost, thus:

Third, though the downward inflexion occurs at the ends of phrases and sentences alike, there is a slight difference between the use of it in each. At a sentence end, since the sense is complete, the inflexion is definite and final. At a phrase-end, however, the downward inflexion should be slight. This slight fall produces a natural rise, so that the sense of incompleteness and expectancy is given. This is particularly important in such 'catalogue' verses as 1 Corinthians 12[28], where there is a tendency to drop the voice as if in completion at every comma.

### PACE

We desire an avoidance of extremes. Nervousness tends to make people speak faster than they normally do; this leads to preachers, especially beginners, speaking too rapidly. On the other hand, a slow ponderous voice is annoying; there is no virtue in slow speech for its own sake. When the congregation begins to feel, 'For goodness' sake, *get on* with it!' the situation is serious.

An average of about 100 words a minute is a good pace. The speed, however, will vary a great deal according to the matter; the important point which the preacher wants to be remembered will be taken more slowly, the less important detail more quickly; there will be greater speed as emotion grips the preacher in an illustration, less speed as the final telling part of the illustration is driven home.

The preacher should not need to learn to vary pace— it should come intuitively of itself. Very often, however, preachers deliberately resist the impulse that leads them to vary it, under the mistaken impression that an even flow of words makes for greater clarity.

Here are the passages we have studied before, with the pace marked in. Notice that there is a certain coincidence between the changes of pitch and pace.

[1]['Jesus saith unto her, [2][Woman, why weepest thou? Whom seekest thou? [3][She, supposing him to be the gardener, saith unto him, [4][Sir, if thou have borne him hence, tell me where thou hast laid him, and I will take him away.

[5][Jesus saith unto her, [6][Mary. [7][She turned herself, and saith unto him, [8][Rabboni; [9][which is to say, Master.'

[1] Slightly faster than average. Not of first importance.
[2] Slower. Gently.
[3] Average speed.
[4] Slower, made so with the weight of sorrow.
[5] Slightly faster than average. Not of first importance, and it leads to a climax.
[6] Very slow. Tense.
[7] Fast, with excitement.
[8] Very fast. Climax.
[9] Slightly faster than average. Not of first importance.

'We hear no more of the young man who sought eternal life and would not give up his wealth. [1][Perhaps, though it is not recorded, he returned to Christ, all his possessions sold. [2][I like to think so. [3][Perhaps he was one of those who stood at the foot of the cross, and saw how Christ fulfilled the advice he had given. [4][But we shall never know.

[5][What the story does tell us, however, is that [6][decency is not enough. [7][Though Jesus loved him, the man went away sad, for in spite of his goodness, he would not give up [8][the one thing which separated him from Christ. [9][Christ's demand is absolute.'

[1] Slower than average. Gently.
[2] Slower still. Suggestion of gentle desire.
[3] Average speed.
[4] Slower than average. Sadness.
[5] Average speed.
[6] Slower than average. Important point.
[7] Average speed.
[8] Slower than average. The beginning of the climax. Important.
[9] Slower still. Vital point. Climax.

The use of pauses is an important consideration most conveniently treated as a subsection of pace.

Obviously, we have to pause for a variety of reasons. Physically, we must pause to take breath. For understanding, we must pause to mark the sense, as frequently at commas and full stops. For emphasis, we pause before the important word or phrase so that it may come with greater force, or after the important point so that it may sink in. Such pauses help speech enormously. Even variation in pace does not make the impression that a good use of pause can create.

The times to pause are (for the sake of the sense) at the end of every phrase (a short pause) ʌ, at the end of every sentence (a longer pause) ʌ, at the end of every paragraph (a still longer pause) Λ, and (for effect) before or after the word to be emphasized △.

Let me give a warning here: pauses, even sense pauses, will not always coincide with punctuation. A very long phrase may need to be broken up. For poor speakers, the shorter the phrases the better. With frequent pauses, even a poor voice can be made tolerable.

We will now try the same passages and see where the pauses should come.

'Jesus saith unto her,∧ Woman,∧ why weepest thou?∧ Whom seekest thou?∧ She,∧ supposing him to be the gardener,∧ saith unto him,∧ Sir,∧ if thou have borne him hence,∧ tell me where thou hast laid him,∧ and I will take him away.Λ

'Jesus saith unto her,△ Mary.△ She turned herself, and saith unto him, Rabboni;∧ which is to say,∧ Master.'

Notice that the pauses are missing at phrase-ends in the last sentence; the rush of words will not permit of them. The needs of effect always take precedence over grammatical considerations, provided that the sense remains clear.

'We hear no more of the young man∧ who sought eternal life∧ and would not give up his wealth.Λ Perhaps,∧ though it is not recorded,∧ he returned to Christ,∧ all his possessions sold.Λ I like to think so.Λ Perhaps he was one of those∧ who stood at the foot of the cross,∧ and saw how Christ fulfilled the advice he had given.Λ But we shall never know.Λ

'What the story does tell us, however,∧ is that△ decency is not enough.Λ Though Jesus loved him,∧ the man went away sad,∧ for in spite of his goodness,∧ he would not give up the one thing which separated him from Christ.Λ Christ's demand is absolute.'

Rhythm must be mentioned here. It is the 'tune' of sentences. This is deep in our nature. In normal conversation most of us use it, but in public speaking, when it is necessary to stress consonants so that they may reach the back, there is a danger that a voice may lose its rhythm. The cure is to recite poetry with a strong rhythm and develop its use.

### VOLUME

How loud? How soft? In general, our speech should be loud enough for the whole congregation to hear the voice without difficulty, but no louder. They should not need to listen.

Many people—especially women—fear that their voices will not reach the back because they are not powerful enough. If they would learn to 'focus' their voices they would not need to fear, but their unhappy method of overcoming their doubts is to try to force more power from the throat. As we have seen, this is impossible, and the result is that the voice becomes harsh in tone, and less audible instead of more so.

The average person, with very little trouble (consisting of breathing exercises) can make himself perfectly audible in a large church *without effort*. The 'without effort' is very important, as we saw when we considered the importance of ease as a preliminary to all speech.

The voice that is too loud is almost worse than the barely audible one; at least the latter makes people attend raptly in order to hear, but the former makes them restlessly anxious to avoid the over-loud voice's hammer-effect.

As pace and pitch must vary, so must volume. For special effects, and these will be rare, very loud or very soft volume has its use. A very loud phrase jars the nerves of the congregation; a whisper forces their attention. We are justified in using these devices only for the strongest reasons. Otherwise, the volume should be matched to the needs of the congregation.

Here are the same passages, with extreme changes of volume marked.

'Jesus saith unto her, Woman, why weepest thou? Whom seekest thou? She, supposing him to be the gardener, saith unto him, Sir, if thou have borne him hence, tell me where thou hast laid him, and I will take him away.

'Jesus saith unto her, [1][Mary. She turned herself, and saith unto him, [2][Rabboni; which is to say, Master.'

[1] Rather soft.
[2] Very loud. Excitement and wonder.

Note that it makes little difference (though I prefer the one I have given) whether the word 'Rabboni' be very loud or very soft; it is the change that matters. Here is another example which illustrates the same point. In this quotation from *Macbeth*, it does not matter whether the last sentence is taken *ff* or *pp*, but it matters very much that there is a marked change: 'Wake Duncan with thy knocking? I would thou couldst.'

Now our other passage.

'We hear no more of the young man who sought eternal life and would not give up his wealth. Perhaps, though it is not recorded, he returned to Christ, all his possessions sold. [1][I like to think so. Perhaps he was one of those who stood at the foot of the cross, and saw how Christ fulfilled the advice he had given. [2][But we shall never know.

'What the story does tell us, however, is that [3][decency is not enough. Though Jesus loved him, the man went away sad, for in spite of his goodness, he would not give up the one thing which separated him from Christ. [4][Christ's demand is absolute.'

[1] Rather soft. Gentle suggestion.
[2] Rather soft.
[3] Louder. Important point.
[4] Louder. Important point.

## EMPHASIS

We have already considered this subject under the headings of pitch, pace, and volume, for variety in each selects the important from the trivial. But the important words of a sentence should also be slightly stressed. In the following one, the important words are italicized.

'Owing to an unfortunate *mistake*, he got the *Express* for *Glasgow*, under the *impression* that it went to *London*.'

The italicized words contain the essential facts, and we can make out what happened from them alone. It is those words which the congregation must retain, though they can forget the rest.

If you feel this is not a matter of much consequence, then try stressing words that are unimportant.

'Owing to *an* unfortunate mistake, *he got into* the Express *for* Glasgow, *under* the impression that *it went* to London.'

The result is ridiculous.

It is curious how often one hears stress misplaced, and more curious still that it most frequently happens in passages or phrases which are very familiar, e.g.'. . . them

D

that trespass *against* us', and 'he said *unto* him', 'God moves in a mysterious *way*'—all these stresses are misplaced.

To stress every word is to stress none, but it is by no means uncommon for preachers, especially when talking to children, to overstress, on the assumption that what they have to say will all become clearer. This irritating habit can also be heard, not infrequently, from women on Children's Hour on the Wireless.

There is another reason for using stress with caution. The simple sentence, 'He said she was beautiful', seems incapable of more than one interpretation, yet it is necessary only to stress each word in turn to find an enormous variety of meaning.

Note that these ironic stresses are heavier than normal sense-stresses.

*He* said she was beautiful. (But nobody else could see it).
He *said* she was beautiful. (But what he thought was another matter).
He said *she* was beautiful. (But as for her sister . . .).
He said she *was* beautiful. (But that was 30 years ago).
He said she was *beautiful*. (Normal sense).

Without using any extra devices (e.g. an ironic pause before 'beautiful' and a 'flat' treatment of the last word, which would contain the implication 'He should get his eyes tested!') stress alone can alter the sense completely.

It is worth-while experimenting with simple sentences, altering the stress and so changing the sense. Here are two.

Why did you ask him that?
After the Reverend John Smith arrived, the leading tenor left.

Emphasis is also used to contrast words and phrases. The Bible is full of examples. The story of the Prodigal Son is a striking one.

'Lo, these many years do I *serve* thee, neither *transgressed* I at any time thy commandment: and yet thou never gavest *me* a *kid*, that I might make merry with my friends: but as soon as this thy son was come, which hath devoured thy living with harlots, thou hast killed for *him* the *fatted calf*.'

Not all the stresses have been put in—only those which show the contrast. Other obvious examples, often used in the pulpit, are: 'Whom God hath *joined together* let no man *put asunder*.' 'I desire *mercy*, and not *sacrifice*.'

St Matthew 25³¹⁻⁴⁶ contains a whole series of contrasts. In Revelation 21 occurs a famous passage which contains difficult stresses. In Verse 1, heaven and earth occur twice each, but each is stressed only the first time. Here it is:

'And I saw a new *heaven* and a new *earth*: for the *first* heaven and the *first* earth were passed away.'

Here are our earlier passages with the stresses underlined. There are, of course, no innuendoes here; the stresses (and they are always slight) are to assist the understanding.

'Jesus saith unto her, Woman, why weepest thou? Whom seekest thou? She, supposing him to be the gardener, saith unto him, Sir, if thou have borne him hence, tell me where thou hast laid him, and I will take him away.

'Jesus saith unto her, Mary. She turned herself, and saith unto him, Rabboni: which is to say, Master.'

'We hear no more of the young man who sought eternal life and would not give up his wealth. Perhaps, though it is not recorded, he returned to Christ, all his possessions sold. I like to think so. Perhaps he was one of those who stood at the foot of the cross, and saw how Christ fulfilled the advice he had given. But we shall never know.

'What the story does tell us, however, is that decency is not enough. Though Jesus loved him, the man went away sad, for in spite of his goodness, he would not give up the one thing which separated him from Christ. Christ's demand is absolute.'

Finally, it may be necessary to remind the reader that he will not be able to vary his voice convincingly by working out beforehand where the changes should come. The examples I have given merely show the necessity for the variation. With these as a guide, the reader should be able to make variation a habit, a natural device which does not need slavish preparation.

# CHAPTER VII

## Manner

MANNER is important. The impression we make as we walk into the pulpit, for example, will last.

There is, or should be, a mixture in our manner of humility and pride. On the one hand, we should be humble as very poor instruments of God's Word; on the other hand, we should be proud of the Word itself. There is, therefore, humility in so far as we represent ourselves, pride in so far as we represent God. If either of these two emotions predominates, the result is unfortunate.

If we crawl into the pulpit like a worm, with an apologetic grin, as some preachers habitually do, we suggest, not humility, but inferiority; if we march into the pulpit, nose high, with an expression of superior contempt on out faces, we suggest, not pride in our great task, but arrogance. Fright can make us leave either of these false impressions. One man, painfully nervous, shambles in with a fatuous smile and shaking limbs; another, under the same anxiety, counteracts it by a poker-face and rigid limbs.

Controlled ease leaves the right impression—an upright carriage, but upright without effort; an easy manner, but not a careless one. The aims, then, of the Preacher, are to appear, and to be, *at ease* and *dignified*.

### GESTURE

Some preachers employ gesture—the use of the body to assist the voice—a great deal; others never employ it. About its advisability it is unwise to generalize, for gesture is a very individual thing; it is an expression of personality.

Used effectively, it can add much to a voice; used badly, it is intolerable.

I have heard men who, having listened to great preachers, assumed that because the great man raised his forefinger to emphasize points, or always took a step forward at a climax in his sermon, this device contained the secret of his greatness and must be copied. To be effective, however, a gesture must be completely natural—virtually unconscious—and it cannot be imitated.

I once saw a man attempt to use such a gesture. At a climax in his address he suddenly flung out an awkward arm and, not knowing how to get rid of it, remained for some considerable period, obviously embarrassed, trying to dissociate himself from the limb which jutted from his side, the fingers splayed out like a toast-fork.

Only use gesture if you must. If you feel you can do without it, then you would be most unwise to attempt what is unnatural to you. If you feel your limbs longing to add weight to your words, then make sure that the gesture you make

(a) Has meaning. This rules out, of course, such irritating habits as fingering your tie, playing with the front of your gown, or scratching your head. Ugly mannerisms annoy a congregation.

(b) Is in complete union with your words.

(c) Is graceful. It can still be vigorous, but it should never be awkward, or ugly, or distracting. Grace is associated with ease, and once again the prime factor in all speech is seen to apply to gesture also.

## RELATIONSHIP WITH THE CONGREGATION

This only concerns us here in so far as it affects the voice. There are two particularly unpleasant voices to avoid—

a patronizing one and an arrogant one. Nobody wishes to sound either patronizing or arrogant, but both come out in the voice as symptoms of the fright we mentioned earlier.

The first will be considered at greater length in the chapter on 'Speaking to Children'. It consists in over-emphasis and slow delivery, and frequently has a physical manifestation in the form of an inane grin. To use it is the quickest way of alienating the congregation.

The second usually (though it can take other forms) consists in woodenness of expression, too great volume and an 'affected' pronunciation of vowels, e.g. 'nevah' for 'never'. This is the next quickest way of alienating the congregation, who come to church of their humility and find any suggestion of pride in a preacher a violation of their trust. It is considered in greater detail in Chapter XII under 'The Clerical Voice'.

# CHAPTER VIII

## *Imagination*

THERE was a time when preachers with imagination were common. Very often they were itinerants and only preached the same few sermons with variations throughout their lives. They were unlettered, and the sermons may have lacked clear theology and construction—but they were great sermons. What they lacked in all else they gained in imagination. The preacher, in a flood of passionate words, would pour out his testimony to the people. Every word was red-hot with his message. His purpose was contained in every fiery syllable—to compel others to follow his Master.

Today we are better educated. Our theology is more sound; our sermons have a better construction, and they are often aptly illustrated. But you will seek far before you hear a sermon take wings of imagination and soar. We are refined, and shrink from vulgarity. From the mouths of many preachers today comes an apology, not an apologia. The sermon may be admirable on paper; but we are preachers, not writers, and the Gospel is not a news bulletin, however well it is read. We are afraid of our emotions, as if the source of our religion were only in the intellect, though if we really believed that it was, we should find ourselves in the hell of Swift's insane admiration of the Houyhnhnms.

Reason is not enough. We do not convince by reason, however cogent; it is only when reason is joined by emotion, when imagination takes the lead, that we convince. Imagination should be the master both of meaning and sound. It should join them and make them one by its own power.

We know what we have to say; we know how to say it. Now let imagination set it on fire!

'Nymph, in thy orisons be all my sins remembered.' Read that aloud. Now recognize it as Hamlet's words to Ophelia; seek out the context; let your imagination dwell for a while on it; and then read it aloud again. Without the imagination it is a very ordinary line. With it, it is perhaps the most poignant line in all Shakespeare's works.

'Pray you, undo this button.' A prosaic, rather stupid line. Now seek it at the end of *King Lear* and find once again that by the touchstone of the imagination dross becomes gold.

It is no wonder, when we so fear this gift, that by an inverted alchemy the purest gold of all, the message of the Gospel, often becomes base. The voice without imagination is cold with the coldness of death; with it comes warmth and light and colour. Without it our message is uninviting; with it the message beckons. Without it we sound insincere; with it comes conviction. Imagine the flawless voice of the wireless news-announcer delivering—in precisely the same way—a sermon. Technically it is perfect, but technique is not enough. The News *we* announce cannot be given that way.

Some years ago my teacher said to me: 'Your voice lacks warmth—learn this.' 'This' was Romeo's speech to Juliet during the balcony scene:

> But soft! What light from yonder window breaks?
> It is the East, and Juliet is the sun. . . .

I shall not easily forget the acute embarrassment of having to deliver this passionate love-speech before a mixed audience for three weeks until my teacher was satisfied. But I learnt this, that once my self-consciousness had left me and I could say the speech *as if I meant it*, neither the audience nor I found any embarrassment left.

There is no need for us to act our feelings when we preach. The congregation warms to the sincerity of the preacher. If there is no warmth, no emotion, no imagination in our voices, then the people may well wonder why we are preaching at all; but, to the imagination in our words, the people must respond.

Here is a test. I have printed three passages below, deliberately omitting the authors' names. Read them through aloud, without first examining them, then re-read them several times silently, letting the imagination work. Then read them aloud again.

(1) 'And once upon a time, Reader—a long, long while ago —I knew a schoolmaster: and that schoolmaster had a wife. And she was young, and fair, and learned: like that princess-pupil of old Ascham: fair and learned as Sydney's sister, Pembroke's mother. And her voice was ever soft, gentle, and low, Reader: an excellent thing in woman. And her fingers were quick at needlework, and nimble in all a housewife's cunning. And she could draw sweet music from the ivory board: and sweeter, stranger music from the dull life of her schoolmaster-husband. And she was slow to understand mischief, but her feet ran swift to do good. And she was simple with the simplicity of girlhood, and wise with the wisdom that cometh only of the Lord— cometh only to the children of the Kingdom. And her sweet, young life was as a Morning Hymn, sung by child-voices to rich organ music. Time shall throw his dart at Death, ere Death hath slain such another.

'For she died, Reader: a long, long while ago. And I stood once by her grave: her green grave, not far from dear

Dunedin. Died, Reader: for all she was so fair and young, and learned, and simple, and good. And I am told it made a great difference to that schoolmaster.'

(2) 'And the talk, the wonderful talk flowed on—or was it speech entirely, or did it pass at times into song-chanty of the sailors weighing the dripping anchor, sonorous hum of the shrouds in a tearing North-Easter, ballad of the fisherman hauling his nets at sundown against an apricot sky, chords of guitar and mandoline from gondola or caique? Did it change into the cry of the wind, plaintive at first, angrily shrill as it freshened, rising to a tearing whistle, sinking to a musical trickle of air from the leech of the bellying sail? All these sounds the spell-bound listener seemed to hear, and with them the hungry complaint of the gulls and the sea-mews, the soft thunder of the break- ing wave, the cry of the protesting shingle. Back into speech again it passed and with beating heart he was following the adventures of a dozen seaports, the fights, the escapes, the rallies, the comradeships, the gallant undertakings; or he searched islands for treasure, fished in still lagoons and dozed day-long on warm white sands. Of deep-sea fishings he heard tell, and mighty silver gatherings of the mile-long net; of sudden perils, noise of breakers on a moonless night, or the tall bows of the great liner taking shape overhead through the fog; of the merry homecoming, the headland rounded, the harbour lights opened out; the groups seen dimly on the quay, the cheery hail, the splash of the hawser; the trudge up the steep little street towards the comforting glow of red curtained windows.'

(3) 'Let us have no imitation Christian Love. Let us have a genuine break with evil and a real devotion to good. Let us have real warm affection for one another as between

brothers, and a willingness to let the other man have the credit. Let us not allow slackness to spoil our work and let us keep the fires of the spirit burning, as we do our work for God. Base your happiness on your hope in Christ. When trials come, endure them patiently: steadfastly maintain the habit of prayer. Give freely to fellow-Christians in want, never grudging a meal or a bed to those who need them. And as for those who try to make your life a misery, bless them. Don't curse, bless. Share the happiness of those who are happy, and the sorrow of those who are sad. Live in harmony with each other. Don't become snobbish but take a real interest in ordinary people. Don't become set in your own opinions. Don't pay back a bad turn by a bad turn, to anyone. Don't say, "It doesn't matter what people think", but see that your public behaviour is above criticism. As far as your responsibility goes, live at peace with everyone.'

Now that you have tried this test—and I hope you have not cheated by reading on—I will reveal where they came from: the first is from an essay on Education in Girls' Schools in a book called *Day-Dreams of a School-Master*, though, it is, of course, a parenthesis; the second is from Kenneth Grahame's *The Wind in the Willows*; and the third is from the Epistle to the Romans, in J. B. Phillips's translation.

The first forced you, as I was forced when I learnt Romeo's speech, to feel its matter deeply and—unlike Romeo's speech—by a mixture of restraint and irresistible emotion to bring out the tone-colour and with it the beauty of the passage.

The second is just as beautiful, but in quite a different way, and the imaginative mind senses the strange mixture of intense joy and nostalgic sadness. Onomatopoeia makes a strong demand on the voice. Here again, feeling could not be resisted.

The third passage is a portion of a sermon preached— albeit on paper—by St Paul. You might be preaching it yourself. Did you move your congregation? Did 'warm' *sound* 'warm'? Was there patience in 'patiently' and strength in 'steadfastly'? Did you make the beauty of the life St Paul commends appear beautiful to the congregation? Was there peace in 'peace'?

The most precious gift the preacher possesses is his imagination. It was fundamental in his call to preach. In his voice it can compel others to pray. The voice is an instrument which can play many tunes—silver whispers, full, mellow golden tone, brass trumpetings. All are at our own disposal. Imagination shows the way.

# CHAPTER IX

## Speaking to Children

THERE is a very good example of how *not* to talk to children in *Tom Sawyer*. Here it is:

'Now, children, I want you all to sit up just as straight and pretty as you can, and give me all your attention for a minute or two. There, that is it. That is the way good little boys and girls should do. I see one little girl who is looking out of the window—I am afraid she thinks I am out there somewhere—perhaps up in one of the trees making a speech to the little birds. (Applausive titter.) I want to tell you how good it makes me feel to see so many bright, clean little faces assembled in a place like this, learning to do right and be good.'

We are also told that the speaker 'held sacred things and places in such reverence, and so separated them from worldly matters, that unconsciously to himself his Sunday-school voice had acquired a peculiar intonation which was wholly absent on week-days'.

Note the faults—the 'special' voice mentioned above, the patronizing manner, the feeble attempt at humour, the use of words and phrases particularly repellant to children (e.g. 'little'), the repetition of inanities (e.g. 'good it makes me feel', 'do right and be good').

All the faults come from the same root cause—the inability to understand a child's mind. If we are to rid ourselves, therefore, of this type of insult to a child's intelligence, it is worth considering for a moment what children feel and, therefore, how they like to be addressed.

Children are not simple, sweet, and innocent. The more I know of them the more I realize they are complicated, temperamental, and knowledgeable. Every teacher and sensible parent will agree with this. It is therefore fatuous to begin an address to children in a gluey voice, with a winning leer and such a phrase as: 'My dear children.' Young people hate to be patronized. For normal purposes, a children's address should be directed rather above the average age of the children present. So many addresses appear to be delivered to the nursery age (when children can rarely concentrate for more than a minute or two) that those from 8 to 14 have nothing.

It is pertinent here that the drift from the Sunday-schools begins about 13. If neither sermon nor children's address has anything to offer, what can hold them? If you direct your address to the age of 7, few below that age will listen and there is nothing for the older ones to hear. Aim, therefore, at about the age of 12 and the majority will have something to take away.

Not long ago a well-meaning Sunday-school teacher came to preach at the boarding-school at which I taught, and horrified the whole assembly by beginning thus: 'Now, boys, on my way here tonight I passed several things by the roadside. I wonder if you can guess what they were? Can you? Would anybody care to say?' Nobody would. Apparently unconscious of the thrilled silence of horror which greeted this question, the poor fellow went on. 'Now, would somebody care to tell me from the front row? Just call out.' Nobody did. After several minutes' hard work he gave up the hopeless task and told us the answer. A lamp post. By then nobody cared anyway.

We can all remember with loathing the silly people who said to us after a lapse of years: 'My! How you've grown!' What did they expect? And yet this sort of asinine comment is commonplace from the pulpit.

Here is a short selection of fatuous remarks and phrases to children which I have heard recently. The child's reaction is supplied in brackets.

'I had a rather funny experience the other day.' (Probably not a bit funny).

'I wonder what you think.' (You would be sorry if you knew).

'We elder children.' (I'd like to see him climb a tree).

'The very small ones among you.' (That's right, 'small', rub it in).

'Shall we put our hands together?' (No).

'. . . who was a good boy really. . . .' (Probably as soppy as a girl).

'. . . took his little sister by the hand. . . .' (Ugh!)

In church, because it is expected of them, and because children have a deep sense of religious respect, children will sit through this sort of stuff. But try it at school! And that is a good test, for the normal reaction of a child can be judged much better in surroundings which allow that reaction to be voiced.

I have considered this matter at some length because I am convinced that the peculiarly disgusting voice assumed for the benefit of children is the expression of a wrong attitude to the child. Children are merely adults with limitations—limited understanding and limited vocabulary—but they are as swift as we are to resent patronage. Therefore:

(1) Don't use any different voice technique for talking to children. The matter of the address will be different, but the manner should not.

(2) In particular, don't

   (a) Over-enunciate. Children are not deaf; usually their hearing is better than ours.

(*b*) Speak more slowly. If the matter is simple, normal speed should be the rule.

(*c*) Be over-dramatic. If the matter is more dramatic (and it should be) there is no need for it.

(*d*) Use phrases which remind children that they are small and unimportant and ignorant (e.g. 'little', 'my dear', 'when I was as small as you are', etc.)

The much less common fault in speaking to children does not appear particularly in the voice, but for the sake of completeness it is worth noting; it is a complete ignoring of the fact that they are children. This example is a genuine verbatim one I heard recently from a minister—and a distinguished one.

'My-ah-dear children—I am about to tell you-ah-about a name-ah-which to you-ah-will mean very little-ah-but who-ah-to our generation-ah-was a *voice*, so to speak.' I refrain from comment.

Another distinguished scholar whom I know well once preached on the doctrine of the atonement at a Sunday-school Anniversary in a rural area. His faith was beautiful, but his judgement on that occasion was open to doubt.

Neither of these two men understood children. They did not insult them by treating them as morons, but neither did they make any allowance for children's limitations.

The BBC has, I feel, certain faults in this direction which have—as everything else the Corporation does—much influence and many imitators. I have heard people on the wireless speaking to children in precisely the over-sweet sickening way that I have described. Worse—I have heard child-actors in plays for children use saccharine voices which would make any normal and healthy child squirm.

E

A realistic approach to the child, a treatment of him as a normal human being, however immature, would rid us of this rubbish, and might well increase the size of our Sunday-schools.

# CHAPTER X

# Hymns, Prayers, Notices

## HYMNS

THE vast majority of churches have boards on which are the hymn-numbers. Only a few people, therefore (those with poor sight and those who are placed so that the board is not visible), need the number announcing at all. The great performance attendant on announcing hymns, therefore, is often a waste of time.

'Let us commence worship with Hymn Number 406, Hymn Number 406, four-o-six.' Isn't this too much? If the voice explained the number clearly once, that should be enough; only a muffled announcement needs double repetition.

After this the preacher reads out part of the first verse of the hymn. This is an admirable practice when it is used well and when it makes sense. But not infrequently, neither condition is fulfilled.

Obviously it is necessary for it to make sense. Many hymns, and notably those of Charles Wesley, are great poems as well as great hymns. To read the first line or two well can therefore be an essential part of worship, for the hymn-book is a book of meditation second only to the Bible. The sense of the hymn, when it is being read, should be read in its poetic context, which can differ from the sung version. For instance, we sing:

'Hark the herald angels sing' (Tune: BERLIN), but we must *read:*

    *'Hark!*ʌ *The Herald angels sing . . .'*

55

Similarly, we sing:

> '*Give me the wings*ᴧ *of faith to rise*ᴧ (Tune: MYLON)
> *Within*ᴧ *the veil and see* . . .'

but we must read:

> '*Give me the wings of faith*ᴧ *to rise*
> *Within the veil*ᴧ *and see* . . .'

I have occasionally heard hymns made into nonsense by the first line only (or even half of it) being read out. Here are examples:

> '*Through the night of doubt and sorrow—*'
> '*All people that on earth do dwell—*'
> '*God moves in a mysterious way—*'
> '*O for a thousand tongues to sing—*'
> '*Breathe on me—*'

In each of these hymns more needs to be read to complete the sense. If it be argued that the line is read only as a reminder to the congregation, who can complete the sense in their own minds, then the answer is that that is not sufficient justification for reading it. If the hymn is good enough to be in the hymn-book, then it should be good enough to be read as poetry.

If the beginning of the hymn does not make sense, even when two or three lines are read, and the preacher does not wish to read the whole of the first stanza, then it is better to read none. A case in point is, '*From Greenland's icy mountains*', where eight lines must be read, or none.

It is a temptation to write at length of the beautiful poetry in many of our hymns, but it is a temptation which must be resisted. Let the preacher only read them for himself before he announces them, and the words must speak for themselves. There is the trumpet-call of

> '*O for a thousand tongues to sing*
> *My great Redeemer's praise—*'

the joy of
> '*My heart is full of Christ, and longs*
> *Its glorious matter to declare.*'

the sorrow of
> '*O Sacred Head once wounded,*
> *With grief and pain weighed down—*'

the conviction of
> '*Now I have found the ground wherein*
> *Sure my soul's anchor may remain—*'

the courage of
> '*Come on, my partners in distress,*
> *My comrades through the wilderness*
> *Who still your bodies feel—*'

the peace of
> '*My spirit on thy care*
> *Blest Saviour, I recline.*'

What hymns! What an opportunity for the preacher!

Finally, it is worth noting that a knowledge of the 'background' of many hymns can help with the reading. How much a knowledge of the Calvinistic Controversy adds, for example, to the reading of this hymn:

> '*Father, whose everlasting love*
> *Thy only Son for sinners gave,*

*Whose grace to* all *did freely move,*
*And sent Him down* the world *to save.'*

## PRAYERS

Little can be said here. Prayers are so individual and
personal that it borders on effrontery to mention them at
all. One point, however, should be mentioned: if we bow
our heads in prayer, it is doubly necessary for enunciation
and articulation to be very clear. The preacher is advised to
be sure of his audibility when he prays.

## NOTICES

The only quality notices really require is clarity, yet it is
often this that they lack. Among a verbiage of 'all are
welcome' and 'tea will be provided by Mrs Crumpet-
Smith and your dear minister's wife', the essential informa-
tion, the date and time and place, is lost.

It is most important to check all notices before the service with a steward. For one thing, local place-names may
be unfamiliar, and people like them to be pronounced
correctly. For another, the notices are not always clearly
phrased. I have known notices prepared for preachers
which were superlative examples of muddle. Here is an
example of one such.

'In the school-room on Wednesday, the Scouts and Guides
will meet with the Old Folks for a Social. There will be a
concert to follow at 7.30 p.m. The Scouts and Guides will
meet before the Social in their room to prepare. Mr ——
will entertain the Old Folks until then.'

The preacher felt justified in translating this gem—after
exhaustive and exhausting inquiries—as follows:

'On Wednesday evening, from 6 o'clock onward, in the School-room, the Scouts and Guides are to entertain the Old Folks. There will be refreshments and a concert.'

By such means the crooked can be made straight, the preacher can announce clearly what is important, and the congregation can know what arrangements to make.

# CHAPTER XI

# Reading the Scriptures

IT has been said of a few men that they read the Scriptures in such a way that no sermon was needed. But it is a rare gift. So often we tend to read the Scriptures as merely a necessary part of a service, conscious as we do so that the congregation has heard it all before and is not listening very acutely. And yet the crux of our sermon is usually contained in the Scriptures.

What the Bible needs, and what it so often lacks, is the breath of life breathed into it through our voices. It needs drama—by which I do not mean a theatrical approach, which suggests pretence and vulgarity, but an approach which makes it living and real and arresting. We should read as if we had never heard it before, and as if the congregation are to hear it for the first time. It should sound—what it is—eternally fresh and eternally wonderful. Read so, the congregation will hear it again, as for the first time, and thrill at its newness.

There have been those in the past who, considering the Bible as a book apart (which it undoubtedly is) have used a 'Bible' voice, a voice strangled by reverence, which was afraid to speak vividly because that hinted at worldliness. There have been those (and they are still with us) who have used a 'cold' even tone for the Scriptures, possibly as a deliberate reaction against the sin of 'ranting'. If this is the reason, then the pendulum has swung too far. Better a thousand times over-zeal than what sounds like cold indifference. The Scriptures are 'the most valuable thing that this world affords. Here is wisdom; this is the royal Law. These are the lively oracles of God.' These are the words that accompany the presentation of the Bible at a coronation in England.

The Scriptures also contain, considered on literary merits alone, the finest writing in our tongue. The Authorized Version is the greatest literary treasure we possess. What poetry is there that can match the Song of Deborah? What narrative can match the Parable of the Prodigal Son or the Journey to Emmaus?

What a combination! And it is our privilege to read it! What tongue dare presume it? What voice can do it justice? Here if anywhere, we must aim at perfection.

The content of the Bible, since it differs so widely from our normal speech, needs separate consideration. Especially is this true of the poetry. Here are three sentences, any of which might be said from the pulpit.

'Some lady left a green handbag in the gallery last week.'
'In St Paul's own person, Roman, Greek and Jew met.'
'By the rivers of Babylon, there we sat down, yea, we wept when we remembered Zion.'

Each is a statement of fact. In each all the rules of correct speech must be observed. Yet each, as we read it, is quite different. (Try this. If that difference is not clear in your own voice, try again. It should be. Try, if you like, reading the first as you do the last. It should sound ridiculous.) You will find—I am *certain* you will find—that the deep sadness of the third sentence affects every phrase in it, that the lyrical music of the line makes music in your voice, lengthens the vowels, permeates the whole.

The Hebrew poetry of the Old Testament is poetry of a very particular kind. It is highly emotional, intense in its feeling. Whether the emotion be of love or hate, sorrow or gladness, the emotion is concentrated and often over-whelming. Parallelism is its peculiar substitute for rhyme, and this device often makes the poetry more of a chant than anything else. The voice, following the poetry, be-comes musical, and at the high emotional pitch demanded, voice-colour is used as nowhere else. The sound for once takes precedence over the sense, and the sense, usually very simple, is felt rather than expounded.

> 'The beauty of Israel is slain upon thy high places:
> How are the mighty fallen.
> Tell it not in Gath,
> Publish it not in the streets of Askelon;
> Lest the daughters of the Philistines rejoice,
> Lest the daughters of the uncircumcised triumph.'
>
> (2 Samuel $1^{19-20}$)

Here it is—a wail, but of tremendous dignity; wave on wave of sonorous sound; beautiful and simple; intense in its anguish. The voice rises and falls with the ebb and flow of the chant. It feels the lamentation of David, and mourns with him.

Here is a short passage which is—if that were possible—even higher in its emotional pitch. This passage changes from extreme longing to bitter hatred, but both parts demand near-chanting.

> 'If I forget thee, O Jerusalem,
> Let my right hand forget her cunning.
> If I do not remember thee,
> Let my tongue cleave to the roof of my mouth;
> If I prefer not Jerusalem
> Above my chief joy.
> Remember, O Lord, the children of Edom

In the day of Jerusalem;
Who said, Rase it, rase it,
Even to the foundation thereof.
O daughter of Babylon, who art to be destroyed;
Happy shall he be, that rewardeth thee
As thou hast served us,
Happy shall he be, that taketh and dasheth thy little ones
Against the stones.'

Elsewhere, such phrases of pure beauty as 'the shadow of a rock in a dry land' demand the same treatment. We must feel the parched throat and burning feet in the dry land, feel the welcome shade.

Here are a few more. Consider the impossibility of reading such passages in any but the way I have suggested. They are not for experiment; read them with their own intensity, first *feeling* them.

(*a*) 'There is a river, the streams whereof shall make glad the city of God.'

This is the stuff of which poetry is made—intangible, almost incomprehensible, like Blake's, 'O Rose, thou art sick', impossible to explain, but beautiful beyond understanding.

(*b*) 'I am the rose of Sharon,
    And the lily of the valleys . . .
    My beloved is mine, and I am his:
    He feedeth among the lilies.
    Until the day break, and the shadows flee away,
    Turn, my beloved, and be thou like a roe or a young
        hart
    Upon the mountains of Bether.'

(c)  'Hast thou given the horse strength?
      Hast thou clothed his neck with thunder?
      The glory of his nostrils is terrible.
      He paweth in the valley, and rejoiceth in his strength.
      He saith among the trumpets, Ha, Ha;
      And he smelleth the battle afar off,
      The thunder of the captains, and the shouting.'

Can you, could anybody read this without the passion
that inspired it? Mark the man well whose 'Ha, Ha' is
not a trumpet-blast, whose 'smelleth' does not snort with
power; he should not read the Scriptures.

Perhaps the strangest mixture of all, in its emotional
content, is the Song of Deborah, with its paean to God,
and savage exultation in bloodshed. It is a narrative poem.

'Blessed above women shall Jael the wife of Heber the
    Kenite be,
Blessed shall she be above women in the tent.
He asked water and she gave him milk;
She brought forth butter in a lordly dish.
She put her hand to the nail, and her right hand to the
    workmen's hammer;
And with the hammer she smote Sisera,
She smote off his head, when she had pierced and
    stricken through his temples.
At her feet he bowed, he fell, he lay down
At her feet, he bowed, he fell.
Where he bowed, there he fell down dead.
The mother of Sisera looked out at a window, and cried
    through the lattice,
Why is his chariot so long in coming?
Why tarry the wheels of his chariots?

Her wise ladies answered her, yea, she returned answer
to herself,
Have they not sped? have they not divided the prey;
To every man a damsel or two;
To Sisera a prey of divers colours, a prey of divers
colours of needlework,
Of divers colours of needlework on both sides,
Meet for the necks of them that take the spoil?
So let all thine enemies perish, O Lord:
But let them that love him be as the sun when he goeth
forth in his might.'

This passage starts in a gloating triumph, reaching a
climax with the horrible repetition 'he bowed, there he fell
down dead'. Subtly, after a long pause, it begins again
with the mother of Sisera awaiting his return. There is
irony in every line until the colours of the spoil glow over
the scene. Then comes a solemn curse, and the passage
ends in adoration. The love of God is constant throughout the passage, but it takes forms very strange to us.

At the beginning, the voice is strong and sure. With
'he asked water' it becomes quicker, with an underlying
hint of what is to come. It rises exultantly with 'She smote
Sisera, she smote off his head'. There is a pause before
'At her feet he bowed'. Then a complete change. After
the pause, a slower, sadder tone. The two lines beginning
'Why is his chariot . . .' are long, the second plaintive.
The ironic joy of Sisera's mother has an undercurrent of
fear as the voice rises to the description of the spoils.
Then comes another long pause and the execration; with
clipped enunciation, it is spat out. The ending fades softly
and slowly, a complete contrast, until the strength of the
sun is felt at the very end.

Often in the works of the prophets passion raises the torrent of words to a demand for similar treatment.

'Take thou away from me the noise of thy songs; for I will not hear the melody of thy viols. But let judgement run down as waters, and righteousness as a mighty stream.'

This is the angry voice of the God of Amos. To read it without the anger and the command is to make a mockery of it.

Much prose in the Old Testament, and some in the New, has this same quality of intense feeling. It is technically prose, but only technically; it has the spirit of poetry. In the Old Testament, David's lament over Absalom is such:

'And the king was much moved, and went up to the chamber over the gate, and wept: and as he went, thus he said, O my son Absalom, my son, my son Absalom! Would God I had died for thee, O Absalom, my son, my son!'

In the New Testament we have:

'And God shall wipe away all tears from their eyes: and there shall be no more death, neither sorrow, nor crying, neither shall there be any more pain.'

Neither passage can be treated as normal prose. As in poetry, so in such places as these, there is a deeper meaning than the words themselves contain, an elemental feeling which suffuses all, and makes the words speak of the nature of things.

When reading prose narrative (as in large sections of the Old Testament, and in the Gospels and Acts in the New Testament) it is normally sufficient to fulfil all the important conditions of speech technique. Only when the narrative becomes more poetry than prose do we (albeit unconsciously) differ in our delivery.

Most of the narrative portions we read are of the same type as the sentence 'in St Paul's own person Roman, Greek and Jew met', which I quoted near the beginning of the chapter. That gave no opportunity, however, for dramatic reading, and many Bible narratives demand it. Consider, for example, the story of David and Nathan:

'And David's anger was greatly kindled against the man; and he said to Nathan, As the Lord liveth, the man that hath done this thing shall surely die: and he shall restore the lamb fourfold, because he did this thing, and because he had no pity.

'And Nathan said to David, Thou art the man.'

Here is drama. The anger of David should be heard in his words. When his words end, there should be a long pause. Then, quietly: 'And Nathan said to David'. A pause. In a strong, but not a loud voice, the climax should come as a surprise to the congregation as it was a surprise to David. The words 'Thou art the man' should be stark; not an accusation, but a statement of cold fact. There is often greater drama in restraint.

We will now consider a normal portion of narrative. Deuteronomy 34 is a good choice, for the death of Moses might well be read as a lesson, and it contains within it a number of problems.

The chief one is a weak climax; the kernel of it is in verse 5, but an attempt is made to drag out the climax for another seven long verses. One way to solve this problem is to take the climax in verse 5 and read the succeeding two verses parenthetically. Take the first half of verse 8 on a dominant note of sadness, and treat very lightly the weak second half. Stress in verse 9 'laid his hands upon him', for there Moses is central. In the last section stress 'knew face to face' and 'signs and wonders', 'Pharaoh' and the last few words. Only so can a second— if still a weaker—climax be made.

A second problem, though a less acute one, is the catalogue of names in the first few verses. This is very common in the Bible. It is surprising, however, what good reading can make of awkward names; sonorous confidence in the delivery can make them sound remote and wonderful. The emphasis in verses 1 to 4 of this chapter should be on the enormous size of the land God gives Moses. Wonder at the magnitude of the gift can appear in the reading, and the preacher has missed much if the command, 'but thou shalt not go over thither', does not contain God's understanding of Moses' disappointment.

We will consider a second passage, this time one of great difficulty, from St Paul's Epistles. The apostle is often difficult; his overladen prose often creaks in grammar. His thought is intricate and his intellect speeds through problems far more quickly than ours can. Any passage of St Paul is a challenge to the reader.

'There is therefore now no condemnation to them which are in Christ Jesus, who walk not after the flesh, but after the Spirit. For the law of the Spirit of life in Christ Jesus hath made me free from the law of sin and death. For what the law could not do, in that it was weak through the flesh, God sending His own Son in the likeness of sinful flesh, and for sin, condemned sin in the flesh: that the righteousness of the law might be fulfilled in us, who walk not after the flesh, but after the Spirit. For they that are after the flesh do mind the things of the flesh; but they that are after the Spirit the things of the Spirit' (Romans $8^{1-5}$).

The most important preparation for this is to read other translations and commentaries to get the sense of it clear. Even then, however, it is far from simple. Verse 1 is clear enough, the stress being on 'no condemnation', and the contrast between 'flesh' and 'Spirit' being brought out. In verse 2 'Spirit of life in Christ Jesus' leads to 'free from'; in the thought here one 'law' is contrasted against the other 'law', but to contrast the same word would be unhelpful. Verses 3 and 4 border on the impossible, and are a grammatical maze. 'Law' here is contrasted with 'God'. A pause must be taken after 'God', so that from 'sending' to 'for sin' can be treated as an adjectival phrase qualifying 'God', and the verb 'condemned' follow on from 'God'. If it be argued that the sense would be far clearer if it read 'God did, by sending . . .', I agree, but then if we choose to read the Authorized Version we must accept the words as they are. At least, read this way, the gist of the message comes through; the law was helpless, but God, through Christ, condemned sin. The force of the first 'for' in verse 3 is, as in verse 2 'because'; the force of the second 'for' is 'to deal with'. Verse 4 reads on after 'condemned sin'. 'That' means 'in order that'. Verse 5, happily, is well constructed and admirably balanced, flesh and Spirit.

Here is a last passage—Isaiah $35^{8-10}$. This exquisite chapter has one problem. Verse 8 reads 'but it shall be for those'. Who are those? Clearly 'the redeemed'. But there are 28 words separating 'those' and 'the redeemed'; these words talk of men and creatures who are definitely *not* the redeemed, but only careful reading can make this

F

clear. From 'the wayfaring men' to 'be found there' must
be treated as a parenthesis—the voice drops, and the
congregation realizes that the sense is suspended for a
while; the parenthesis, taken at a lower pitch, can still
have variety in that pitch and the beauty of it can still be
brought out. This done, the voice comes back and picks
up the abandoned thread with 'but the redeemed'.

### PRACTICAL SUGGESTIONS

(1) Always prepare thoroughly before reading a passage
from the Scriptures.

- (a) Know what it means. (If this seems obvious, remember St Paul.)
- (b) Feel what the author felt and prepare to read it as
if you were the author.
- (c) Make sure you can pronounce all awkward words
in it, especially proper names. (There is some
variety here; what chiefly matters is that *you know*
that you are pronouncing it right!)

(2) If you feel there is something lacking in your reading
of the Scriptures, persuade a fellow preacher (or, better
still, a group) to read passages aloud with you, each com-
menting on the other's reading. Here are passages suggested for that purpose.

*Old Testament*

*Poetic*

| Psalm | | |
|---|---|---|
| | 47 | of joy |
| | 88 | of sorrow |
| | $42^{1-5}$ | of longing |
| | 91 | of trust |
| | 114 | of power |

| | |
|---|---|
| Psalm 121 | of peace |
| 136 | a problem. Can it be read without sounding repetitive and wearisome? |
| 148⎱<br>150⎰ | Psalms rich in sound. 150, in particular, has musical instruments which can be heard in the voice. |
| Job 3$^{1-10}$ | Job's curse. Bring out the bitterness with the misery. |
| 32$^{6-10}$ | Elihu's intrusion. From self-doubt to confidence. |
| 38$^{4-7}$ | God's reply. |
| 41$^{19-34}$ | Leviathan. |
| Song of Songs 2$^{10-17}$ | A lyrical passage of great beauty. |

## Narrative

| | |
|---|---|
| Genesis 1$^{1-5}$ | The Creation. Mystery over all. The gloomy nothingness before the Creation. |
| 22$^{1-13}$ | The offering of Isaac. Climax in the contrasting verses 10 and 11. |
| 37$^{15-36}$ | Joseph is taken to Egypt. The brothers' hatred and the father's grief. |
| Exodus 14$^{19-29}$ | The crossing of the Red Sea. |
| Judges 11$^{29-40}$ | The Vow of Jephthah. Verse 34 'his daughter came out'; irony of 'timbrels' and 'dances'. |
| Judges 16$^{23-31}$ | The Death of Samson. The strength in 'and he bowed himself with all his might'. |

| | |
|---|---|
| 1 Samuel 18$^{1-9}$ | Saul's jealousy of David. Great contrasts—love, joy, jealousy. The cause and effect of the chant. |
| 1 Kings 19$^{4-8}$ | Elijah in despair. The change from despair to new courage. |
| 1 Kings 21$^{1-10}$, $^{17-20}$ | Naboth's vineyard. Great contrast of character—sulky Ahab, bold Naboth, crafty Jezebel, fierce Elijah. |
| 2 Kings 2$^{23-4}$ | Children and Bears. The tale has no moral value whatever. How should it be read? |
| 2 Kings 5$^{9-14}$ | Naaman healed. Powerful drama. The aristocratic Naaman finds humility. |
| 2 Kings 11$^{10-16}$ | The death of Athaliah. One of the most dramatic stories in the Bible. Contrasting cries of 'God save the king' and 'Treason'. The contempt of 'the way by which the horses came . . .' |

*Prophetic*

| | |
|---|---|
| Isaiah 6$^{1-8}$ | Isaiah's call. A wonderful climax. |
| Isaiah 9$^{2-7}$ | The Prince of Peace. Double antithesis in verse 2; verse 5 savage; verse 6, after a pause, a complete contrast. |
| Isaiah 40$^{1-8}$ | Comfort ye. A series of antitheses. |
| Isaiah 53$^{4-9}$ | The Suffering Servant. Supreme prophetic sadness. |
| Jeremiah 8$^{18-22}$, 9$^{1-3}$ | His Sorrows. Intense suffering, personal and national. |

| | |
|---|---|
| Hosea $11^{1-4}$ | Father's love. |
| Amos $5^{21-24}$ | Righteousness. Burning indignation. |

## New Testament

### Gospel Narrative

| | |
|---|---|
| Matthew $2^{16-18}$ | Herod slays the children. Poetry following prose. |
| Matthew $5^{1-12}$ | The Beatitudes. It is most difficult to avoid repetition in 'Blessed are'. |
| Matthew $14^{15-21}$ | Feeding the Five Thousand. All the wonder is in Verses 20–21. |
| Matthew $17^{1-8}$ | The Transfiguration. Contrast of voices—Peter, God, Jesus. Intensely dramatic. |
| Luke $4^{1-13}$ | The Temptations. The subtlety of Satan. |
| Luke $10^{25-37}$ | The Good Samaritan. The irony of the gentle 'but a certain Samaritan'. |
| Luke $24^{13-32}$ | The Journey to Emmaus. One of the most perfect gems in the Gospel narrative. |
| John $1^{1-14}$ | A difficult passage. Requires very careful reading; correct stresses are vital. |
| John $19^{19-22}$ | The superscription on the Cross. Whatever we make of Pilate's character must appear in his words here. |

John 19$^{25-30}$                The Crucifixion. The suffering
                                of 'I thirst'; the triumph of 'It
                                is finished'.

*Narrative*

Acts 7$^{54-60}$                The death of Stephen. Contrast
                                in the fury of the mob and the
                                peace of their victim, especially in
                                'he fell asleep'.

Acts 19$^{23}$-20$^1$            The riots over Diana of the
                                Ephesians. The indignant crafts-
                                men, the furious rabble, the
                                clever governor.

*Epistles* (including St Paul's speeches in the Acts of the
Apostles).

Acts 26                         St Paul's speech before Agrippa.
                                The dramatic interruption of
                                Festus (verse 24), Agrippa's sym-
                                pathy (verse 28) and St Paul's
                                reply.

Romans 5$^{1-11}$               A difficult passage. Correct stress
                                vital. Many antitheses.

1 Corinthians 13               A very fine passage for reading
                                aloud. Magnificent prose.

Philemon 8–20                  Paul's plea for a runaway slave.

*Apocalyptic*

Revelation 21$^{1-7}$           Poetic prose. A passage of great
                                beauty. Read as poetry.

# CHAPTER XII

# Common Faults and their Cures

IT will be convenient to start with 'types' of bad voices, in so far as such 'types' can be said to exist. The most hated among congregations is without question the so-called

## CLERICAL VOICE

Every syllable is given its full sound value so that when we should say: 'Don't get the idea that heaven is a place where angels merely play harps', we have: 'Don't get the i-de-ah that heav-un is a place where an-gels me-ah-lee play harps.'

The neutral vowel, a very common one in our language, does not exist in this vocabulary. 'The' is more 'Thee'; 'a' is 'ah'; 'actor' (normal pronunciation 'actə' is 'ac-t<u>or</u>'). Other vowels become distorted: 'power' sounds like 'pah', 'fire' like 'fah', 'man' like 'men', 'hand' like 'hend', 'off' like 'awf', and 'office' like 'awfice'. The general impression given is one of unctuous superiority. There is no more infuriating voice to hear.

If you suffer from this fault you are almost certainly not reading this book, for it would never occur to you that there was anything wrong with your voice. If by chance you are, then address your congregation as you would your old head-master and I am sure there will be many more to hear you the following week.

## THE HOLY DRONE

This is usually a result of intoning. It is very tedious to listen to. Its chief characteristic is a lack of variation in pitch and a tendency to lengthen vowels without good reason. To cure this defect, practice in pitch variation (over-compensating at first) should be almost sufficient. Variation in pace and volume should also be practised, as often the three help each other.

The other cause of the Holy Drone, mentioned in Chapter VI, is the anxiety to make every word audible. As we have seen, this is not the way to obtain audibility.

### THE BISHOP'S BOOM

Some men imagine that the only possible voice to use in preaching is a full, rich bass, and that the deeper and louder the voice, the more excellent it is.

The dangers of this are that few voices are really bass anyway, that forcing down the pitch will ruin the tone, and that the desire for deepness often prevents the voice varying in pitch as it should. Worst of all, such voices lose the ends of sentences altogether in a bass growl of incoherence.

People who are made conscious of this fault should take some trouble in finding out their own middle pitch, and resist the urge to boom. Booming, which comes from the throat, is very difficult to understand in spite of its volume. As I have said elsewhere, the voice should be well forward, on the lips and teeth and tongue.

A ponderous manner of speaking is a frequent accompaniment of the Bishop's Boom. Here are two genuine examples which I heard recently; both were uttered without a trace of humour.

'There is a meeting—my dear friends—on Sunday evening at . . . (an open-air site). I do hope—that you can be there. The evening—may be somewhat chilly—and you will perhaps permit me—to remind gentlemen—to take an extra waistcoat—and ladies—ah—the equivalent.'

'Spring is with us again. Last Sunday—I walked past trees—which were barren—and lifeless. Today—as I walked here, nature—to speak in the vernacular—hit me in the face.'

The cure for this aspect of the Bishop's Boom is the cultivation of a sense of humour. Practice of the above example might meet the need.

### THE SUNDAY-SCHOOL DROOL

This wide-spread speech fault is commonest in young ladies and senior men, and is used largely in talking to children. It is mentioned here mainly for the sake of completeness, for I have considered it at length in Chapter IX, but as this voice is sometimes heard at normal services, we must note it.

The symptoms are over-enunciation, over-use of pitch variation, a vacuous smile, and a very condescending manner. Symptomatic introductory words are 'now' and 'well'.

The cure here is a true assessment of the intelligence of others.

### MELANCHOLIA

This fault is not uncommon, and is wearying to hear. Usually the pitch varies very little, the pace is slow, and there is a repetitive downward inflexion. Tone is flat and dull. The imagination is not used, and all sentences are spoken in the same lifeless way.

The cure is hard work on exercises for variation of pitch, pace, and power, and a consideration of the importance of the imagination.

### THE GOLDEN VOICE

A golden voice should be an asset. It can, however, be a liability when the owner of the voice is conscious of its beauty and obviously enjoys listening to it. A congregation does not go to church to listen to a beautiful voice. This particular fault is, however, rare.

All the faults mentioned above are not so much caused by one particular defect as by a general attitude. The faults we must now consider are particular defects which need particular treatment. Reference has been made to some of them elsewhere. Here the aim is a brief identification, and suggestions for cure.

## INDISTINCTNESS

There are several causes.

The speaker may not give sufficient vigour to consonantal sounds. It is these which make for clarity. Too much tone on vowels and too little on consonants can make speech unintelligible at the back of a large hall: for example, there is little difference between the following two sentences if enunciation is not clear.

'He went to York where, in the fog, he lost his way.'
'She went a walk wearing the frock she lost in May.'

Blur the consonants, give full vowel value, and judge for yourself. Try also these:

| | |
|---|---|
| sent to | send to |
| with | width |
| first town | furze-down |
| faction | fashion |
| breadth | breath |
| revues | refuse |
| disease | decease |
| rainstorm | reins torn |

Another cause of indistinctness may be the inability of the speaker to project his voice to the back of the church.

The speaker must learn to 'focus' his voice both physically and mentally. If the trouble is breathing, and it may well be, hard work is necessary on the breathing exercises in Chapter III. Incorrect production of tone would produce the same effect, and in that case a consciousness of the importance of producing the voice on the lips and teeth and tongue might produce the cure.

### OVER-CAREFUL SPEECH

This is the reverse of the last habit, and though less serious, is very irritating. A frequent accompaniment of it is unnecessary distortion of the lips which can render the preacher comic. Usually, it is necessary only to know that one is doing it to be cured.

If the speaker first acquires the ability to speak correctly, the method by which it is done should be forgotten. A speaker cannot concentrate on what he is saying if he is always worried about how to say it. Good speech should be a habit. Over-careful speakers are ineffective.

### LACK OF VARIETY

Since variety is the principal means of maintaining interest, lack of it is a serious deficiency. Chapter VI is entirely concerned with variety, and the person who feels he lacks it should study that chapter with care. It must be emphasized that variation should sound natural, or it is worthless. This can only happen when the use of it has become habit.

### UNPLEASANT TONE

The speech organs are very sensitive, and any abuse of them inevitably leads to bad tone. There are two kinds of bad tone—throaty and nasal.

Throaty tone is usually caused by misuse of the speech organs and the attendant damage this causes between the larynx and the pharynx (the back of the throat). Shouting, speaking from the throat, and infection of the organs, catarrh, over-use of the one voice-register, rigidity of muscles of the throat—all these can lead to throaty tone. The cure is rest and a clear understanding of the principles of voice production.

Nasal tone has a different kind of origin. In properly produced speech (apart from the three sounds to be mentioned in a moment), the soft palate is raised to shut off the nose from the throat; the air can then come through the mouth only and, assuming all other conditions of voice production are observed, the tone is pure. If the soft palate is lowered, air is emitted through the nose, and this occurs when we make the three nasal speech-sounds— n, m, and ng. These are the *only* speech sounds in which the soft palate is lowered (see consonant table); and if we lower it for others, we produce nasal tone.

Nasal tone is the result of a weak soft palate, the weakness permitting air to come through the nose, partially or entirely. Nasality is cured by strengthening the muscles of the soft palate. Unfortunately it is a long process and results come slowly. Yawning and whistling have been found to help, but the commoner methods are these.

(1) Test all sounds for nasality, and work from the non-nasal to the nasal.

(2) The vowel ĭ is most commonly free. If this is so, work from it to other vowels. If even this vowel is nasal, work from the consonant z.

(3) The man with nasal tone clearly cannot tell that his soft palate is lowered. But he will be able at least to feel it (and even, perhaps, to control it) if he alternates the

sounds 'ng' and 'ā'. The explosion between the sounds is the movement of the soft palate.

These are the principles governing the cure of this fault. Since, however, as I have suggested, the cure is a slow process, and it is difficult to work alone, speakers with this handicap are strongly recommended to consult a speech therapist.

## LISPING

This is more common in children than among adults. It is mentioned briefly in Chapter V.

Here, in detail, is the correct position for the S sound. The tongue-tip should be just drawn back from the upper teeth ridge; the tongue should be grooved and the sides of it should touch the upper teeth. The breath is forced along the groove of the tongue and passes over the tip of it. Lisping occurs when the tongue-tip is advanced too far, or when it is not sufficiently vigorous to 'point' the sound.

Exercises which make the tongue-tip more pliable are helpful. Here are two useful ones:

(1) Place a finger between the teeth and attempt to sound 'th' vigorously with the tongue pressed against the finger. Take away the finger.

(2) Work from 't' to 'ts' to 's'.

## STAMMERING

Most stammerers are not consistent in the places where they stammer. The cause is incorrect breathing. Jerky breathing and tension in muscles (both of which are frequently caused, as we have seen, by nervousness) both lead to this state.

The cure begins with the mental approach and relaxation.

Then come breathing exercises and a gradual building-up of self-confidence which can banish the problem entirely.

Few speakers, obviously, are bad stammerers, but many would-be speakers never become so because of this difficulty.

## STUTTERING

As opposed to stammering, which is more general, stuttering means finding difficulty with certain consonantal sounds. As with stammering, nervousness is the usual cause. Practice of the particular consonantal defects should be avoided, as this is likely to have the effect of strengthening the muscles which are being misused.

The oldest, and best remedy, is singing. 'If you can't say it, sing it', then say it in a sing-song way, and so return to normal speech by this route. As immediate aids, the following suggestions may help.

(1) As many stutterers find an initial explosive sound difficult, they may find relief by interposing a half-vowel before a difficult consonant, e.g. 'primitive' becomes 'a primitive' or 'ap-rimitive'. Practice can make the 'a' so short as to be inaudible.

(2) Since it is through nervousness and jerky breathing that stuttering arises, breathing exercises will be a help. Even a bad stutterer can, with practice, learn to breathe deeply, and speak out easily on the outgoing breath. This both makes short phrases easy, and aids breath-control.

## *Finally*

THE steward was hurrying to church, though it was only ten past ten and the church fifty yards down the street. He was anxious to avoid the situation which had arisen last week, when twelve people were sitting in a pew intended for eight and others were sitting in the aisles, making it difficult for the organist to get to the front.

By 10.15 he had arranged for extra chairs to be placed outside the open church doors, for the disused gallery to be opened, and for two extra officials to be instructed in dealing with the crowds. By 10.30 he had dealt with the first mad rush and was hoping that, with only half-an-hour to go before the service, his arrangements would be adequate.

They were not. At 10.45 he opened every window in the church, knowing that on as pleasant a day as this, the minister's voice would be able to reach the several hundred people who were sitting on the tomb-stones, regretting they had not come earlier.

Five minutes later a hum of excitement started outside the church and was taken up inside. The minister was arriving. The crowd awaited with eagerness that organ voice, those mellow ringing tones, that voice which, it was said, could make the hardiest sinner find his knees. . . .

A loud cough made the steward jump. He woke up. Groping, he found his watch under the pillow. Only eight o'clock. He stifled a yawn and focussed his thoughts. Sunday. Mr Smith to preach. With luck there might be three in the congregation, including the organist. They would have to sit in the front row, of course; Smith's voice might be audible there. But then, wasn't it a 'distance-enhances-the-view' sort of voice, anyway? The less you heard of it the more you liked it. What cannot be cured must be endured. And arming himself with such thoughts, the steward fell asleep once more. . . .

There *is* a cure!